GWYDIR CASTLE

CASTLE

*A History
and Guide*

PETER
WELFORD

GWYDIR
PRESS

GWASG
GWYDYR

Foreword

WHEN WE ACQUIRED GWYDIR in the autumn of 1994, neglect and decay were everywhere apparent. Consumed by damp and partly roofless, the place had quietly sunk to its knees; meanwhile the authorities looked on and bemoaned the fate of this 'problem house'.

We were both in our twenties then, and, armed with little more than a deep love of history and a romantic sensibility, we raised a bank loan and began to tackle the rather daunting challenges presented by Gwydir's restoration. Those long days of hard work – and the many bizarre adventures we had along the way – were set down by Judy in her acclaimed book *Castles in the Air* (Judy Corbett, Ebury Press, 2004).

During the past 28 years of restoring the house and gardens, we have become accustomed to the sights and sounds of restoration work: an endlessness of scaffolding, code 7 lead, lime-wash and mortar; of stonework renewed and stonework repaired – the eye-watering cost of every small detail, from leaded lights to handmade nails. This wonderful old house still provides us with an inexhaustible supply of problems, but equally of delights. While fresh excitements and challenges continue to present themselves, the muscular work is now largely behind us, and the place is, structurally at least, in good order once more.

Gwydir's timeless atmosphere and melancholic beauty have been an inspiration to people for hundreds of years. A previous guidebook to Gwydir (from around 1924) contains a passage which, more than anything else, expresses for us the essence of Gwydir's importance in an increasingly unsettled and confusing world: 'The ubiquity and ceaseless activity of the modern builder, ravaging and despoiliating everywhere, is here held at bay; and the delightful castle and its gardens remain a heritage of the past, for the solace and mental delectation of the present generation, and maybe of those to follow'.

Our philosophy here is very much in accord with these sentiments. We have tried, wherever possible, to approach the restoration of Gwydir with a light hand and a ready ear: listening to the place has been a very important part of the restoration process.

Ancient houses like Gwydir are the sum of their parts, historical as well as architectural. But in addition they evolve a particular frequency over the centuries, which is specific to nowhere else. Gwydir has its own time, its own smell, its dense and layered atmosphere, which amounts to the metaphysical equivalent of its archaeology; this represents, in short, the soul of the house. It is this soul, this 'spirit of place' that we have tried to safeguard and nurture. It is a vulnerable quality all too easily destroyed. We have tried to keep Gwydir's ancient humours and harmonies in balance; and if that means there are a few cobwebs here and there, or that the wisteria finds its way occasionally through an upstairs window, then so be it.

The many messages of support and encouragement we have received from visitors continue to move and inspire us in our work here at Gwydir. The unfolding restoration has been an enormous challenge which, with the exception of a small grant from Cadw, we have funded ourselves. The challenges continue, most

'*Really, upon my consideration of the seate of Gwidder, I conclude it to be the best place in Wales, and inferiour to few in England.*'

Thomas Bulkely, 1661

pertinently in the form of increased river flooding, which has begun to erode both the castle and its important gardens in recent years.

We are well aware of the great privilege it is for us to live our lives here. It is a particular pleasure, therefore, for us to be able to continue to welcome friends and strangers alike to share in the special qualities of this remarkable place. As a friend once wryly observed, we live in a house that keeps us both fit and poor. In coming to visit Gwydir you are making a direct contribution towards its upkeep and restoration, and as such we are (ourselves *and* Gwydir) hugely appreciative. We hope you find this guidebook helpful, and that you will be inspired by Gwydir's history and tranquility during your visit.

Peter Welford & Judy Corbett

Origins of name and early history

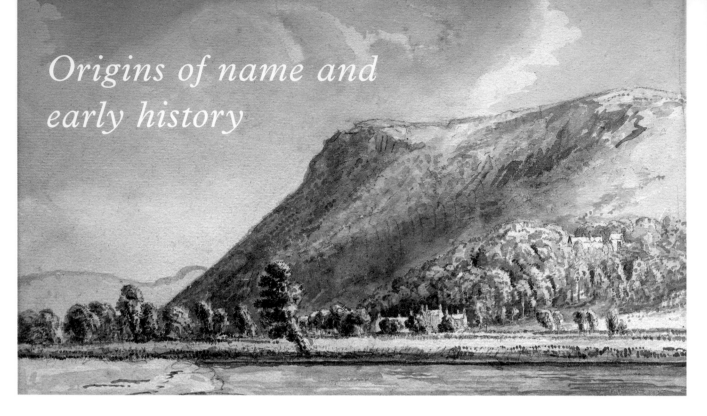

GWYDIR CASTLE is situated on the western side of the River Conwy opposite the historic market town of Llanrwst. It lies beneath the Carreg-y-Gwalch, or 'Falcon's Crag', on a slight rise overlooking the river's fertile and eponymous valley.

The origins of the name are obscure. Thomas Pennant, the eighteenth-century antiquary, suggested a derivation from *Gwaed-dir*, the Bloody Land, in reference to the succession of early battles fought on this site. A less romantic – though more probable – alternative is *Gwy Tyr*, or Watery Land. Even now the low-lying fields are subject to occasional flooding, and the natural moat that results may to some degree explain the choice of this location, rather than the more apparently defensive hilltop above, for the siting of Gwydir.

Distant view of Gwydir beneath the Carreg-y-Gwalch: watercolour by Moses Griffith, 1777.

Gwydir has been given many names in the half-millennium of its known history: Gwydir House; Gwydir Mansion; Gwydir Court; *Plas*, *Plasty*, and Fort. By the early nineteenth century its name had stabilised and since then has always been known as Gwydir Castle. Ironically, one of the earliest bardic descriptions of the house refers to it as *Castell Wedir* – Gwydir Castle – so there is a pleasing circularity here.

This land was notable already in the Dark Ages for the large number of battles and skirmishes fought between the various rival princes and their forces, here in the heart of the Vale of Conwy. Of these the most significant were in 610 and 954, remembered in Welsh history for the unprecedented scale of their slaughter.

The Coetmors

B Y THE LATE medieval period some form of high-status house had evolved on the site. At the time of the Caernarvonshire survey of 1352, Gwydir was in the possession of the Coetmor family, a significant regional dynasty showing lineal descent from the royal house of Gwynedd. Gwydir's first recorded owner is traditionally held to be Hywel (or Howel) Coetmor, a commander in the Hundred Years' War during the reign of Richard II.

Various Coetmors, in fact, appear to have served in the French wars, including Griffith ap Dafydd Goch, Hywel's grandfather, who is said to have fought at the battle of Poitiers under the Black Prince in 1356, and whose fine stone effigy of c.1385 survives in St Michael's Church, Betws-y-Coed. Though the traditional claim that Hywel was one of the captains at the battle of Agincourt in 1415 remains unproven, there is reason to believe that he served as one of Owain Glyndwr's senior commanders during the Glyndwr revolt, which began in 1400. As such, it is possible that he took part in the battle of Shrewsbury in 1402 against King Henry IV. He is shown in the full plate armour of c.1415 in his funerary effigy, preserved in the Gwydir Chapel which adjoins Llanrwst church.

Hall of Meredith.

Hywel Coetmor's tomb effigy,
Gwydir Chapel, Llanrwst.

The first Wynn:
Meredith ap Ieuan ap Robert

Meredith ap Ieuan ap Robert, from his funerary brass in Dolwyddelan church.

S OME TIME around 1490 Gwydir was sold by Hywel's great-grandson to Meredith ap Ieuan ap Robert. Meredith (or Maredudd) emerges as a man of remarkable vision and courage. He founded the powerful Wynn dynasty, which for much of the sixteenth and seventeenth centuries dominated the North Walian political scene, with Gwydir at the centre of a vast and lucrative estate.

Meredith was born around 1460. He was descended from Roderic, third son of Owain Gwynedd, the Warrior King (d.1169), grandfather of Llewelyn ap Iorwerth, known as Llewelyn the Great. By the fourteenth century the family had established itself in Eivionedd in South Caernarvonshire, near Criccieth. Meredith's formative years were dominated by violence and bloodshed at a time not only of civil war, but also of continuous internecine feuding. His father, Ieuan ap Robert, was a loyal supporter of the Lancastrian faction during the Wars of the Roses, and had jointly led a successful attack on the Yorkist stronghold of Denbigh in 1466. The resultant sacking and burning of the town led King Edward IV to dispatch the Earl of Pembroke as a reprisal to waste the Conwy Valley, a major centre of Lancastrian sympathy. This he carried out with devastating efficiency; Ieuan died as a result of a plague which ensued, aged only 31.

Meredith inherited a bloody legacy, and, faced with the prospect of – as he put it – either having to kill or be killed by his own friends and kinsmen, he decided to leave his ancestral estates. In the late 1480s he settled, while still in his mid-twenties, in Nantconwy, obtaining the lease of the royal castle of Dolwyddelan. Over the next two decades he managed to consolidate and control an area which hitherto had gained a reputation for total lawlessness. His early life was recorded in a colourful and swashbuckling account by his great-grandson, Sir John Wynn, the 1st Baronet, who wrote a history of the Wynn family around 1600. Much of what we know about Meredith and the early Wynns stems from this famous account. We are told that, having gained

many enemies and being paranoid about assassination, Meredith demolished Dolwyddelan church, rebuilding it in a more strategically defensible location, at the same time rebuilding the semi-fortified house at Penanmen, a mile equidistant from both Dolwyddelan's church and castle. His bodyguard of twenty tall longbowmen went everywhere with him, and he could call at any time upon a small private army (seven score) of well-equipped and mounted followers.

Meredith apparently went twice to Rome, and is recorded as having rendered the king great service in France; he participated in the Battle of the Spurs and was a 'considerable commander' at the siege of Tournai in 1513. Having gained control of Nantconwy, he settled at Gwydir around 1500, and from then on this, rather than Dolwyddelan Castle or Penanmen, served as the principal seat of the Wynns. He appears to have remodelled the pre-existing hall range of the Coetmors, and built the adjoining quasi-military Solar Tower, which forms the most imposing part of the present complex. The partial survival of a moat and associated wall, recorded as visible still in the early nineteenth century, may relate to this period, or equally to an earlier phase of occupancy under the Coetmors. Whatever the date and context of these now vanished elements, they suggest that the early house had at least some (notionally) defensive aspects, and that the early bardic references to 'castle', or 'fort', should not be seen as entirely fanciful.

Dolwyddelan Castle.

Meredith died at Gwydir in 1525, having fathered some 27 children with three wives and four 'concubines'. He lies buried in his church at Dolwyddelan, his brass depicting him, appropriately, in a fashionable (and expensive) suit of plate armour. Lauded by the bards, his reputation was built upon his ready sword and 'spear of flashing fire'; yet his equal linguistic facility in Welsh, English and Latin was also regarded as notable among his contemporaries.

> *'Meredith's reputation was built upon his ready sword and spear of flashing fire'*

John Wynn ap Meredith

EREDITH'S son, John Wynn ap Meredith, spent his youth shadowing his father and learning at his side. Both are recorded as having attended Sir Rhys ap Thomas's famous tournament held at Carew Castle, South Wales, in 1506. Regarded as Wales's last great medieval tournament, it was held by Sir Rhys to commemorate his elevation to the Order of the Garter. The 16-year-old John was given the honour of commanding one side of the 'melee' against Sir Rhys's own son, and was described as 'a hopeful gentleman of good towardliness . . . of a fair expectation and clearly spirited'.

John further consolidated the estates and greatly enlarged the house, incorporating material from the demolished Cistercian abbey of Maenan, dissolved c.1538. Along with other Welsh gentry families at the time of the Acts of Union under King Henry VIII, he adopted an anglicised surname, Wynn, meaning 'fair'; and his latinised initials, I.W. (Iohannes Wynn) can be seen in several places, notably in the spandrels of the main gate arch, together with the date 1555.

John Wynn served as High Sheriff of Caernarvonshire in 1545 and 1557, achieved considerable prominence in local government and was elected to Parliament. He died in 1559 and was buried in the family church at Dolwyddelan. Like his father before him, John was a blend of warrior, administrator and cultivated gentleman. Also a Latinist, and a great patron of the bards, he was celebrated by them as 'the father of his people' and 'the prince of his lands'. The bard Gruffudd Hiraethog went further: 'You are the soul of the country, whose wings are widely spread over regions, a sagacious and beneficient person to whose court the men of two provinces come to pay their respects'. During his lifetime Gwydir evolved into a spacious courtyard house, which was likened by Morus Dwyfech to the courts of Camelot and Windsor. He further proclaimed that this 'fortress of dressed stone . . . will last until Judgement Day, like immovable St Paul's'. (We have yet to see whether this prophecy will prove correct.) Among his many achievements, John Wynn is remembered in Welsh folklore as the man who finally destroyed the notorious 'Red Bandits of Dinas Mouthwy', a well-organised and powerful criminal militia who had long terrorised the region.

Earliest surviving view of Gwydir, c.1720.

*'John Win ap Meredith dwellith at
Gweder at ii bows shottes above
Conwey toune, on the ripe of the river
Conway: it is a pretty place.'*

John Leland, c.1536

Maurice Wynn
and Catherine of Berain

İN 1559 JOHN WYNN'S SON Maurice succeeded to the estate and assumed political and regional prominence in his turn. As well as serving as High Sheriff and MP for Caernarvonshire, he held a variety of additional official posts, including Commissioner for the Suppression of Piracy, and Commissioner of Musters. He was closely associated with Queen Elizabeth's favourite, Robert Dudley, Earl of Leicester and Baron Denbigh, with whom he later clashed over a number of local political matters. His third wife, one of the most glamorous former inhabitants of Gwydir, was the Queen's ward and cousin, Catherine of Berain, known as '*Mam Cymru*' (the Mother of Wales).

Various legends are associated with the glamorous and mercurial Catherine. An early tradition claimed that she poisoned each of her four husbands in turn by pouring molten lead in their ears while they slept; she then buried their bodies in the orchard at Berain.

Thomas Pennant, the eighteenth-century antiquary, recounted the well-known tale of her pursuit by and eventual marriage to Maurice Wynn. The story goes that Maurice proposed to Catherine as she came out of Whitchurch, the old parish church of Denbigh, having just buried her first husband, John Salusbury. Maurice, however, found himself outmanoeuvred: Sir Richard Clough, his rival, had proposed to her on the way in. Catherine declined Maurice's offer, but kept his hopes alive by saying: 'Should I have to perform the same sad

Catherine of Berain, 'Mam Cymru', d. 1591,
in a portrait dated 1568 (National Museum of Wales).

Plas Mawr, Conwy, built by Maurice's younger brother Robert Wynn between 1576 and 1585 (from a nineteenth-century illustration by A. & H. Baker).

duty that I perform here today, I will happily consider your suit'. Within a few years Sir Richard was dead and Catherine moved into Gwydir as Maurice's third wife.

Catherine's son by an earlier marriage, Thomas Salusbury, married Maurice's daughter Margaret Wynn in a powerful dynastic alliance designed to fuse the fortunes of these two great Welsh families. These aspirations, however, ended in tragedy when Thomas was executed for treason in 1586 for his part in the famous Babington Plot to assassinate Queen Elizabeth. As with his father and grandfather, Maurice was a significant patron of the bards, and served as one of the commissioners for the 1568 Eisteddfod held at Caerwys.

His support for and encouragement of the Welsh language came at a significant time when North Wales was experiencing its own cultural and linguistic renaissance. He famously identified the son of one of his tenants, William Morgan, as intellectually promising, and duly had him schooled at Gwydir together with his own children, before putting him through Cambridge. Bishop Morgan, as he subsequently became, went on to produce the first Welsh translation of the Bible, and is celebrated as one of the pioneers of the modern Welsh language. It is significant that this important Welsh figure received his earliest education in Latin, Greek and English at the hands of the chaplain-cum-schoolmaster at Gwydir; and the sophisticated and lyrical quality of his written Welsh – long celebrated – evidently derived from his early years as a scholar here. Gwydir's famous library was consulted by many of the early Welsh humanist scholars.

Maurice Wynn's brother Robert served Sir Philip Hoby, soldier, diplomat and friend of Titian, until his master's death in 1558. He then returned to Wales and built himself a 'worthy plentiful house' called Plas Mawr in Conwy; conceived in Flemish Renaissance style, this survives as arguably the most complete and important Elizabethan town house in Britain.

Sir John Wynn
1st Baronet

MAURICE'S ELDEST SON, John, inherited the estates in 1580 at the age of 27. Sir John, the 1st Baronet as he subsequently became, emerges as one of the most significant and charismatic personalities of early modern Wales. Evidently a man of exceptional forcefulness as well as ability, he was feared and respected equally by his contemporaries. As patron of the arts and of learning, writer and antiquary, tireless public servant and entrepreneur, he dominated the cultural and political landscape of the region for over 50 years. In one of many bardic tributes he is acclaimed as 'a second Moses of Gwynedd'; other contemporary accounts refer to him as 'a discreete person . . . of wisdom and fidelitie', praising his 'good diligence and careful consideration'. But above all it is his industry and integrity that become apparent when one examines his (ample) correspondence; together with a constant sense of the importance he placed on the exhortations of his personal motto: *Nec Timet, Nec Tumet* – 'Neither fear nor vanity'.

Educated at All Souls', Oxford, and the Inner Temple in London, Sir John's sharp wits and legal training ensured that Gwydir and its estates more than prospered during his tenure as head of the family. Through careful husbandry and business acumen he turned Gwydir into one of the largest and most profitable estates in the principality, with lands extending across all five of its northern counties. An inheritance worth a comfortable £200 *per annum* grew under his stewardship into one worth over £3,000, the contemporary equivalent of an earl's income.

Sir John Wynn, 1st Baronet (1553–1627).

Urbane and courtly, he was highly regarded by the Queen's favourite the Earl of Leicester, and counted Sir Frances Bacon, the Lord Keeper, among his many friends and supporters. The public offices he held were many, including High Sheriff of Caernarvonshire, Merionethshire and Denbighshire, Member of the Council of the Marches of Wales, Deputy Lieutenant of Caernarvonshire, and MP. After a long-awaited knighthood in 1606, he was first in Wales to receive the Baronetcy at its instigation in 1611. He married, in 1576, Sidney, daughter of Sir William Gerard, Lord Chancellor of Ireland, Vice-President of the Council of the Marches and Recorder of Chester. In Sir John's own words, she was his 'chief prop and stay' and their long and happy marriage produced twelve children, for two of whom (plus a son-in-law) he managed to obtain knighthoods within his own lifetime.

> *'Avoid the alehouse, to sytt and keepe drunkards company ther, being the greatest discredit your function can have.'*
>
> **Sir John Wynn's instructions to his chaplain**

Lady Sidney Wynn, d. 1632.

During his time at Gwydir he continued to enlarge and embellish the house, turning it into an enormous double-courtyard mansion; much of this work was subsequently swept away around 1820, when the castle was returned, more or less, to its early sixteenth-century size. Sir John described himself as 'an continual builder', and among other projects built an ambitious new 'lodge' or summer-house on the natural plateau above Gwydir. This 'Upper House', or Gwydir Uchaf, was completed in 1604 and still survives, though extensively rebuilt in the nineteenth century. The grammar school and almshouses that he built and endowed in Llanrwst (1611–14) have also survived.

Of his many writings, his *History of the Gwydir Family* and his *Memoirs* are best known. Written around 1600 and contained within his 'Great Book', they were published to great antiquarian acclaim in 1770 and are regarded as among the most important surviving accounts of their date. These important works, together with the vast body of letters and early manuscripts relating to Gwydir and the Wynns (some 3,000 documents) have made a major contribution to the understanding of Tudor and Stuart Wales.

Sir John's success (and ruthlessness) in business and politics gained him powerful friends, but also inspired great jealousy among his regional contemporaries. 'Yow must lerne to know your frends from your enemyes', he wrote to his eldest son in 1604, '. . . who to take, who to leave & who to hearken after . . . for be assured, the envious hatefull man feirs naught, & wyle do yow mislike when he ys able: as I shall leave yow frends, so also enymyes'. The rather distorted reputation history has given Sir John originates with those 'enemyes', who compelled him to defend himself in the Star Chamber and the Court of Chancery accused of all manner of villainy, fraud and corruption. In all, between 1580 and 1611 he was drawn into at least 27 lawsuits. Proud and ambitious though he doubtless was, he had a highly developed sense of personal and family honour, which he zealously defended – even against the bishops of St Asaph and Bangor when whey were rash enough to cross him. Sir John died in 1627 at the age of 73; he lies buried in the Wynn Chapel in Llanrwst, beneath an alabaster monument commissioned in London thirteen years earlier.

Gwydir Uchaf, the 'Upper House', completed 1604 (from a drawing of 1684).

Sir Richard Wynn
2nd Baronet

IN 1614 SIR JOHN'S ELDEST SON, also Sir John, died of the plague at Lucca in Italy while on the Grand Tour, aged only 31; it is thought that he had converted to Catholicism. His brother, Sir Richard, inherited Gwydir together with the Baronetcy on old Sir John's death. He accompanied Prince Charles as Groom of the Bed Chamber and Gentleman of the Privy Chamber on his expedition to Madrid in 1623, and wrote an amusing account of the journey and his impressions of the Spanish court. These impressions seem to have been largely negative. Writing to his father he maintains 'Castile and Aragon together are not worth one of the worst counties in Wales. The Welsh mountains are but mole-hills, but their barrenness is most fruitful in comparison with Spain. Henceforth I will believe anything reported of another country rather than go and see it.'

He is traditionally said to have brought twelve Cedar of Lebanon saplings back with him from Spain, which were planted at Gwydir to commemorate the wedding of King Charles I and Henrietta Maria in 1625 (three of these apparently survive and can be seen on the Cedar Lawns). He was subsequently appointed the Queen's Treasurer and Receiver-General, and became a devoted servant and friend to the royal couple.

In parallel with his royal posts, Sir Richard sat as MP (variously for Caernarvon, Ilchester, Andover and Liverpool), and his duties inevitably kept him more or less permanently in London. Here he had a fine house

Sir Richard Wynn, 2nd Baronet (1588–1649).

('London House' in the fashionable Strand), and lived the lavish life of the courtier. He also had a further country seat, near Brentford, which had come to him through his marriage with Lady Ann Darcy. His visits to Gwydir were consequently all too rare, and Owen and Maurice, his brothers, were deputed to run the Welsh estates in his absence.

Though serving as an MP when civil war broke out in 1642, his sympathies were naturally royalist, and he continued to represent the King's interests within the 'court' faction in parliament until his position became untenable. Already in April 1641, perhaps sensing how things would unfold, he sent cartloads of weapons up from London to Gwydir ('powder, muskets, pikes, head-pieces, swords, bows and arrows to defend (my) self if the times prove bad'). Although realistically too old for active service, there is evidence he nevertheless carried the rank of colonel, and there are some oblique references in contemporary correspondence to his involvement in military affairs. He also served their majesties in other ways, giving, among other things, over £8,000 of his own money to the Queen when she was in need. There is evidence that since the 1630s Sir Richard had been undertaking clandestine missions on behalf of both the King and the Queen, and was evidently a trusted confidant. One commission from the King, given to him for an unspecified journey abroad, entitled him to 'command any man, horse or vessel in the King's name'.

Sir Richard built the imposing Wynn memorial chapel onto Llanrwst church in 1633, which houses a series of spectacular monuments and brasses to Sir John and his descendants, including Sir Richard's own (by the important court sculptor Nicholas Stone). He also built the famous *Pont Fawr*, the triple-arched bridge over the Conwy linking Llanrwst with Gwydir via the 'Gwydir Avenue'. This is dated 1636, and since at least 1753 has been attributed to the architect Inigo Jones, whose family are supposed to have originally been tenants of the Wynns, and in whose capacity as Court Architect he would have had frequent contact with Sir Richard at Whitehall.

Parish church of St Grwst, Llanrwst: the Wynn Chapel, exterior and interior.

Sir Owen Wynn
3rd Baronet

S IR RICHARD died childless in 1649, in the same year as King Charles's execution. The Baronetcy consequently passed to the third brother, Sir Owen. Schooled at Westminster and Eton, he entered the Chancery under the patronage of Archbishop Williams, the Lord Keeper, whose niece, Lady Grace, he married in 1624. Sir Owen appears to have been something of a recluse and spent much of his time at Gwydir engaged in alchemical experiments; a list of his many alchemical books has been

Sir Owen Wynn, 3rd Baronet, d. 1660.

preserved. He was described by his brother as having a 'bushy beard which he always wore careless'. During the Civil War, Sir Owen looked after Gwydir in his brother's absence. Although a royalist, neither he nor his other brother Maurice took part in active service, though both acted as Commissioners of Array, with responsibility for the provision of supplies, arms, horses and powder for the royalist army.

It is traditionally believed that King Charles I visited Gwydir in 1645 after his defeat at the battle of Rowton Moor and his subsequent flight into Wales. Whether this story is true cannot now be proved. What is recorded, however, is that after the royalist defeat at the battle of Denbigh Green on 1st November 1645, the surviving cavalier horse 'in number 900 fled towards the mountains, and fell that night upon the house of Sir Richard Wynn (Gwydir), where they stayed five days, and on going, rifled the house'. During this period Archbishop Williams, the Lord Keeper, stayed frequently with his niece at Gwydir while he conducted

Reconstruction of Gwydir as it might have appeared around 1620
(from a painting by Peter Welford).

16

his bitter feud with Major-General Sir John Owen over who should control Conwy for the King. It was presumably this rivalry, together with the rancour that existed between the Wynns and Sir John Owen, that led to his troops plundering 200 head of Gwydir cattle. In the same year a Captain Thornton and his men were dispatched to garrison Gwydir. Owen writes in a letter to his brother that 'they were not unruly and the officer was extremely courteous'; his wife Grace, however, took a different view, and thought them 'very rude'. What precisely happened at Gwydir during these turbulent years remains unclear, but a surprising quantity of musket and pistol shot of the period have been unearthed in the gardens.

Sir Richard Wynn
4th Baronet

Sir Richard Wynn, 4th Baronet, d. 1674.

prisoner in Caernarvon Castle, and only his mother, Lady Grace's charm offensive against the puritan Colonel Madryn, eventually secured his release. Sir Richard married Sarah, daughter of the doughty Sir Thomas Myddleton of Chirk Castle, erstwhile parliamentarian Major-General turned staunch royalist and supporter of the Restoration. Sir Richard served as MP for Caernarvonshire and Chamberlain to Charles II's queen, Katherine, to whom he reputedly presented a large pearl found in the River Conwy. He built the delightful chapel at Gwydir Uchaf in 1673, a year before his death of the plague; his wife, Lady Sarah, had also succumbed to plague only two years earlier.

SIR OWEN'S SON Richard, later the 4th Baronet, served as a royalist captain under his cousin Colonel Roger Mostyn, chiefly in the garrisons at Flint and Chester. Later, in 1659, he took up arms again when he participated in the ill-fated royalist rising known as Booth's Rebellion. For this he spent a period as a

> **'Gwydir, where worthy entertainment and most cordial welcome were never found wanting.'**
> **Sir Roger Mostyn, 1670**

Sir John Wynn
5th Baronet

Sir RICHARD lacked a male heir, so the vast Gwydir estates passed to his young daughter Lady Mary, 'Mally' as the family affectionately called her. She married Robert Bertie, Lord Willoughby de Eresby in 1678, aged 17, but died only eleven years later. The marriage had been arranged by her formidable grand-mother, the mercurial Lady Grace, widow of Sir Owen, the 3rd Baronet. Bertie subsequently became 4th Earl of Lindsey and 1st Duke of Ancaster and Kesteven, and went on to have two further wives. Thus the direct link with Gwydir was severed, and from then on it became secondary to the chief Ancaster estate, centred on Grimsthorpe Castle in Lincolnshire.

The Gwydir Baronetcy could not be transferred through the female line, so it was continued in a junior branch represented by a grandson of Sir John, also called John. He, the 5th and last Baronet, founded the Wynnstay family, subsequently the Williams-Wynns, and died at the age of 91 in 1719. Sir John led an adventur-ous life, from his youth as a royalist captain during the civil war to his later years as 'the richest man in Wales'. A wit, duellist and gambler, he once acquired the castle and manor of Shrawardine in Shropshire on the back of a snail race. In his eighties, a former school friend, now a bishop, proclaimed: 'Ah, Sir John. In your youth the devil was very great with you.' 'Would that the devil were half so great with me now, m'lord!' replied Sir John. He was buried in Ruabon church, under, as the antiquary Philip Yorke observed, 'a mass and massacre of marble, ludicrous to look at'.

Sir John Wynn, 5th and last Gwydir Baronet, d.1719.

As the seventeenth century progressed, the core family increasingly used Gwydir Uchaf as their preferred residence, while Gwydir proper, perhaps already then being regarded as rather old-fashioned, appears to have been inhabited largely by junior family members, guests and the (extensive) household. When the Duke of Beaufort, the new President of the Council of the Marches of Wales, made his famous progress in 1684, it was at the 'Upper House' that he was put up and entertained.

Gwydir in the eighteenth and nineteenth centuries

THE BERTIES, and subsequent lords Willoughby de Eresby, held the estate throughout the eighteenth and nineteenth centuries, though until the 1820s rarely used it as a residence. A fire is said to have destroyed part of the complex during the time of the second duke, Peregrine Bertie, in the early eighteenth century. By the end of the century, when antiquaries like Thomas Pennant and Richard Fenton were taking a renewed interest in the house, it was tenanted by farmers and was becoming increasingly dilapidated. The fame of the discovery and publication, in 1770, of the 1st Baronet's *History* and *Memoirs*, ensured a steady stream of antiquaries and painters, who threaded their way down the valley to see Gwydir for themselves.

Several recorded their impressions, including the Revd Richard Warner, who, in 1797, wrote: 'The ancient family house of the Gwydirs . . . is now a farmhouse, and all its pristine glory is extinguished; time was, however, when it made a figure, and boasted a magnificence which no other noble residence in Wales displayed.' Other antiquarian travellers similarly lamented its increasingly dilapidated – if picturesque – state, to which surviving topographical sketches and watercolours appear to testify.

In 1809 Priscilla, 20th Baroness Willoughby de Eresby, inherited the Gwydir and Grimsthorpe estates. Her husband, Sir Peter Burrell, was raised to the peerage in 1796 as the 1st Lord Gwydir. Although Gwydir itself remained tenanted during their lifetime, their impressive London town house in Whitehall happily sequestered the

Main picture: watercolour of Gwydir from the north-east, painted in 1797 by John Wells.

Inset: Sir Peter Burrell, 1st Lord Gwydir, a contemporary caricature by Richard Dighton, 1816.

View of the gatehouse: watercolour by John Buckler, 1810 (National Library of Wales).

View of the Gatehouse and Hall Range from the courtyard: engraving after a drawing by L. Francia, 1812.

Watercolour showing the courtyard, by John Britain, c. 1800.

'Gwydir House ... gives you an idea of the old house of defence,
by the strong gates and surrounding moat.'

John Byng, 1793

name; Gwydir House, as it is still called, currently serves as the headquarters of the Welsh Office.

Between 1820 and 1822 the subsidiary ranges around the main courtyard were demolished and a decade later work began under Peter Robert, 21st Baron Willoughby de Eresby and 2nd Baron Gwydir, on improving and restoring the remainder. Various cosmetic alterations were carried out by 'the good Lord Willoughby' during this period, and a new west wing, housing a kitchen and services, was erected, copying the style of the original work. It is probable that Sir Charles Barry, the eminent nineteenth-century architect and designer of the new Palace of Westminster, was involved in this work, since plans of his survive showing a proposed west wing, as well as the Knot Garden in the form of a Tudor rose, which now embellishes the main courtyard.

The restoration of Gwydir Castle was commemorated on the main gateway: on the left of the arch is the (original) incised date 1555, while to the right can be seen the added 'Rd 1828' (restored 1828).

For much of the remaining nineteenth century the castle served as an occasional summer residence for the family, while Gwydir Uchaf became the residence and office of successive agents of the vast estate. This had been reduced in size at the end of the seventeenth century, but still amounted to some 78,000 acres in 1895. Members of the discerning public continued to be admitted 'to admire the state rooms', a tradition established already in the eighteenth century.

View of the main courtyard: watercolour by John Buckler, 1810 (National Library of Wales).

Inset, left: Peter Robert, 21st Lord Willoughby de Eresby and 2nd Lord Gwydir.

Inset, right: the Knot Garden in the main courtyard.

'Gwydir Castle, one of the most ancient in this country: how grievous was our disappointment to find this old fortress situated in the only recess where a fine view could possible be avoided.'

Catherine Sinclair, 1833

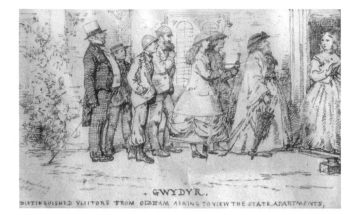

Nineteenth-century visitors to Gwydir: a sketch
(by kind permission of Lady Willoughby de Eresby).

The Willoughby de Eresbys were great estate improvers, and the churches and villages of Trefriw, Betws-y-Coed and Dolwyddelan, among others, saw much restoration and rebuilding during the second-quarter and mid-nineteenth century.

In 1895 the estate was sold to a cousin, Charles Wynn Carrington, subsequently Marquis of Lincolnshire, who continued at Gwydir until 1921. A prominent statesman and friend of the royal family, he regularly entertained foreign and colonial dignitaries at Gwydir, and in April 1899 the Duke and Duchess of York, later King George and Queen Mary, stayed here as his guests.

The Duke and Duchess of York's visit, 1899
(Lord Carrington can be seen standing on the far left).

Recent history

In 1920 the castle was sold to the high society art dealer Lord Duveen, and a year later its historic contents were dispersed in a much-publicised two-day sale. The following year a fire broke out and gutted the Solar Tower, leaving it roofless; a subsequent fire in the west wing made the place untenable and it was abandoned, remaining unoccupied until 1944. In that year a retired bank manager named Arthur Clegg bought the castle and, together with his wife and son, began a programme of restoration which was to last some twenty years. Some of the work carried out during these years was, in retrospect, very much of its time. However, the immediate post-war period saw the destruction of countless large houses of this type, and in fairness it is probable that without Mr Clegg's enormous energy and drive, Gwydir would now be little more than a romantic ruin.

The present

The present owners, Peter and Judith Welford, bought Gwydir in 1994 and immediately implemented a full-scale restoration and conservation programme, necessitated by years of neglect. A variety of complex structural problems was encountered, and the restoration has been informed by much careful interpretive analysis.

Lost treasures

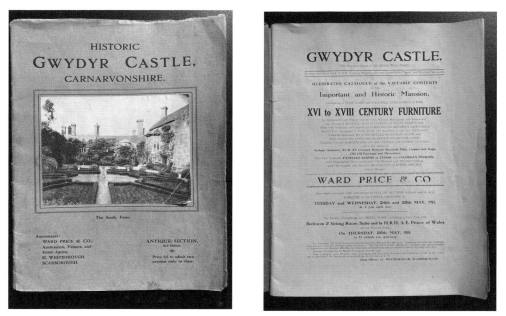

The Gwydir sale catalogue of 1921.

ONE OF THE MOST significant aspects of the ongoing restoration has been the return of some of Gwydir's furniture and fittings which were dispersed in the 1921 sale. Of these the most significant has been the repatriation and reinstallation of the famous Dining Room. This room, with its fine seventeenth-century oak panelling, carved doorcase and heraldic fireplace, was bought by William Randolph Hearst, the famous American newspaper magnate. On his death in 1956 it was bequeathed to the New York Metropolitan Museum of Art. Here, incredibly, it remained in storage, still in its fourteen unopened packing cases. In 1995, negotiations for the repatriation of this room to Gwydir began between the present owners and the Metropolitan Museum. Eventually, and with the generous support of Cadw (the Welsh heritage body), the room was purchased and finally repatriated to Gwydir, after a 75-year American exile. Restoration work on the north (Dining Room) wing, including reinstallation of the returned elements, was finally completed in the summer of 1998; the restored Dining Room was opened by HRH The Prince of Wales in July 1998.

Traditionally attributed to Inigo Jones, the room ranks as one of the most important examples of its type and date and includes a 12-foot-high baroque door case with twin Bernini-inspired solomonic columns, together with a highly important frieze of early polychromed, gilded and embossed leatherwork. The search for the missing 'Oak Parlour', with its c.1540 linenfold panelling and 1597

The 'Oak Parlour', photographed in 1921.

'Caesars' overmantel' continues. Also purchased by Hearst, it was initially installed in his New York apartment block, 'The Clarendon', where elements are shown in interior photographs taken in 1929. Removed probably already by 1936, the current whereabouts of this second famous Gwydir room remain unknown.

Two further important Wynn pieces have returned recently, both due to the enormous generosity of an American benefactor. These are the famous Elizabethan 'Wynn Table', with its remarkable heraldic carving, and the 'Wynn Chest' of Sir Owen, the 3rd Baronet, and his wife Lady Grace, carved with their arms.

The search for items relating to the history of Gwydir Castle continues. Ultimately we hope to locate and reassemble as much as possible of the collection dispersed in the 1921 sale. Apart from the Dining Room, table and chest, we have been fortunate in securing the important portraits of Sir Richard and Sir John, the 4th and 5th Baronets, as well as various early topographical watercolours of Gwydir. We have also recovered the fine Elizabethan heraldic fireback which can, once more, be seen in the Hall of Justice after an 80-year 'exile'.

Tour of the house

THE MAIN GATE bears the date 1555 and the initials and arms of John Wynn ap Meredith, the son of the builder of the present house. The lion and the eagle which appear as supporters are found repeatedly in the spandrels of the entrances at Gwydir and represent two of the three heraldic devices of the Wynn family, the third being the *fleurs de lis* motif. The gates retain their decorative ironwork which is largely original. To the right of the gate is the former gatehouse, where the porter lodged; essentially mid-sixteenth century, it was reduced in height in the early nineteenth. It currently provides accommodation for holiday lettings.

The Great Court with its early nineteenth-century knot garden was originally a cobbled service courtyard enclosed on all sides by storeyed ranges. The early nineteenth-century demolition of many of the subsidiary elements of Gwydir effectively reduced the castle to its late medieval/early Tudor core. The large Solar Tower, facing the gate across the courtyard, is one of the earliest sections of the castle, and, together with the adjoining Hall Block, is of c.1500; the storeyed porch with the prominently carved eagle is a two-phase addition of the mid and later sixteenth century.

Beyond the semi-octagonal stair tower with the gothic tracery windows is the entrance to the castle via the Lower Hall.

The Lower Hall

This range belongs to the primary building phase and by around 1500 had evolved into its present form. The Lower Hall originally served the dual purpose of lesser hall and kitchen, with buttery and pantry spaces beyond a former cross-passage at the far end; mortising evidence in the far ceiling beam shows this. The original post-and-panel partition now appears repositioned and partly mutilated against the end wall. The stopped-chamfered ceiling beams feature pyramid-shaped broach stops, an early stylistic feature. In one section a series of finely moulded beams has been inserted in a former (though not original) staircase opening. These beams are of early Tudor character and are probably reused from the former parlour. The fragments of plasterwork are the surviving remains of an extensive scheme of decorative

Elizabethan plasterwork carried out at Gwydir probably in the 1570s. Sadly, the majority of this was destroyed in the early twentieth century, although it is well recorded in nineteenth-century photographs.

In the nineteenth century the room was known as the 'Servants' Hall, or Old Kitchen', suggesting that for much of its history it had served the same purpose. The passage at the fireplace end leads to the Hall of Justice.

The Dining Room

This famous room was created in the mid-seventeenth century for Sir Richard Wynn, 2nd Baronet of Gwydir, friend and servant to King Charles I. In the centre of the carved fireplace overmantel can be seen an heraldic cartouche with the arms of the Wynn baronets; the cornice above bears the date 1642. In the 1820s embellishments were added by Lord Willoughby de Eresby, which included the provision of the fine late seventeenth- or early eighteenth-century leather frieze, probably reused from elsewhere in the castle. Of London workmanship, the frieze is an extremely rare and important survival of its type. It is lavishly decorated with gilding, silvering, complex stamping and polychromy; in its time it would have represented one of the most costly forms of interior decoration available.

Having been sold in 1921 in the famous Gwydir Castle sale, the room was repatriated in 1996 and reopened by HRH The Prince of Wales on 25th July 1998.

The Hall of Justice

This space, extruded in the angle between the Hall Block and the Solar Tower, is traditionally said to have served as a manorial court at the time of the 1st Baronet, Sir John Wynn (1553–1627). It is called the 'Justice Hall' or 'Hall of Justice' in nineteenth-century descriptions; a cellar lies beneath. The carved door to the left of the sixteenth-century fireplace leads to the Dining Room.

Returning to the Hall of Justice, a small passage at the far end leads to the Solar Tower.

The Solar Tower

The Solar Tower contained the most important rooms of the early house. This ground floor space served as a parlour for much of its time, with the Great Chamber above. Still called the Oak Parlour at the time of the Gwydir Castle sale in 1921, this room formerly had fine linenfold panelling of c.1540, and an important poly-chromed and gilded Elizabethan plasterwork overmantel (known as The Casesars' Overmantel), dated 1597. The latter was originally in the chamber above the gateway, and was rc-crcctcd in this room on thc rcmoval of thc upper floor of the gatehouse c.1820.

In the **glazed display case** can be seen a few of the many archaeological artifacts found at Gwydir over the years. Beneath the large window are displayed various sections of dressed and carved stone found here, including **fragments from Maenan Abbey.** Among them are several pieces of late thirteenth- or early four-teenth-century date which were originally part of the fabric of an important Cistercian monastery, originally located some three miles away. After the Dissolution of the Monasteries (1536–8) the abbey was demolished and the building material became available to the Wynn family. Some of this was incorporated into the mid-sixteenth-century additions at Gwydir, most notably the spiral staircases serving the Solar Tower and the Hall Block.

Ascending either the medieval stone spiral stair or the later oak stair, one reaches the Great Chamber on the first floor.

The Great Chamber

Originally the Solar (from the Latin *solarium*, or sun room), this became the Great Chamber during the Elizabethan period when the glazed bay was added above the porch. At the same time the ceiling was removed to create an imposing double-height room. The ceiling was subsequently reinstated, but in doing so cut across the line of the Elizabethan arch giving onto the oriel. This was the most important reception room in the house, where polite entertaining and dining took place.

An inventory taken in 1627 records the following furniture and furnishings: 'A standing cupboard with a table and leaves, four pieces of hangings, two turkie carpets, a greene carpett with a greene silk fringe, thirteen turkie wrought chairs whereof one with arms, six turkie wrought stooles, eight turkie wrought cushins, one long window cushin, six old turkie wrought cushins with Queene Elizabeth's name on, a crimson inbrodered chaire with two stooles belonging to yt, a needle work chaire, four wooden chaires, six pictures and a map.'

The Stair Head

The stair head leads to an L-shaped corridor, the so-called Ghost Passage. Here one can peer into one of the **early Tudor lavatories.** These were the original paired garderobes which served the Solar and upper chambers of the tower. They were accessed from the other side, this opening being a later alteration. The toilet shaft can be seen below and originally opened into a drain. Such garderobes tended not to be used much after around 1600, with portable 'close-stool boxes' being more usual in the seventeenth century (several of these are mentioned in the 1627 inventory). The shaft and drain were excavated a few years ago and some of the finds are displayed in the vitrine in the Solar Hall (ground floor). They include part of the original oak plug or lid to the loo seat, as well as a hinge and lock, presumably from a former door.

The Ghost Room

Formerly called Sir Richard Wynn's Chamber, after the 2nd Baronet (d.1649), this has been furnished in the style of the mid-seventeenth century. Sir Richard was the Chief Gentleman of the Bedchamber to King Charles I and Treasurer to the Queen, Henrietta Maria. At the end of the Ghost Passage one enters the main, or 'great' hall, the so-called Hall of Meredith.

The Hall of Meredith

This was the main or upper hall and was referred to as the Hall of Meredith, after the founder of the Wynn dynasty, already in the late seventeenth century. Its wide, arched-braced collar truss roof is a good example of the late medieval Conwy Valley type and has characteristic cusped windbraces in two tiers. It is possible that this roof relates to the earlier, Coetmor house, and that Meredith merely re-modelled a pre-existing hall range. The access is via a stone newel stair similar to that in the Solar Tower, and also an addition of c.1540. The ceiling to this stair tower, with its moulded joists, crenellated brattishing and carved, foliated bosses is particularly worthy of note. The shield bearing the three eagles of Prince Owain Gwynedd was the chief component of the arms of the Wynn family at Gwydir.

At the passage end is a small recess created within the thickness of the enormous chimney breast, which serves the lower hall fireplace. This is traditionally said to have been used as a priest's hide during the Catholic persecutions under Queen Elizabeth in the 1580s and 1590s.

Although there is no direct evidence to suggest that the then owner, Sir John Wynn, held Catholic beliefs, his father Maurice certainly did, and his wife, Lady Sidney Gerard, came from a staunch 'old faith' family. In addition to this, Sir John's brother-in-law, Thomas Salusbury, was hanged, drawn and quartered as one of the chief conspirators in the Babington Plot of 1586, which aimed to kill the Protestant Queen Elizabeth and replace her with the Catholic Mary Queen of Scots.

In 1585 it became an offence of 'high treason' for a Catholic priest to minister in England and Wales. If a priest were to be caught by the searchers he could expect no less than torture and execution; those found harbouring priests often shared this fate. The provision of such secret hides was therefore an understandable necessity in the recusant houses where priests were given shelter.

At the far end of the hall is the entrance to the Panelled Parlour.

The Panelled Parlour

In 1921 this room was referred to as King Edward's Room, named after King Edward VII who visited Gwydir, together with Queen Alexandra, as the guest of Lord Carrington (subsequently the Marquis of Lincolnshire). Gwydir was Carrington's home from 1895 until 1920. During his time here the castle had many illus-trious guests, including the Duke and Duchess of York (subsequently King George V and Queen Mary), the Duke of Cambridge (son of Queen Victoria) and Prince Edward of Saxe-Weimar. Oak trees were planted by these and others between 1899 and 1911 in the so-called Royal and Statesman's Gardens, located beyond the present car park.

The rush matting is hand woven in England. It is an accurate copy of the type of woven matting popularly used in the sixteenth and early seventeenth centuries.

Gwydir's ghosts

IN COMMON WITH many buildings which have enjoyed such a rich history, Gwydir has acquired a reputation for being one of Wales's most haunted houses.

Perhaps the most significant (and currently most widely reported) of the ghosts is that of a young woman who haunts the north wing and the panelled corridor between the Hall of Meredith and the Great Chamber. In the nineteenth century the room behind the panelling was called the 'Ghost Room'. A white or grey woman was said to have been frequently seen in the room and the adjoining passageway, accompanied

by a foul smell of putrefaction. The apparition continues to be seen or felt from time to time, and some claim to have been touched on the shoulder while at the same time experiencing a considerable drop in temperature. In addition, the extraordinary smell associated with the sightings continues to be experienced in the same passageway.

While we are not certain of the ghost's identity, an account published in 1906 provides a vivid (and rather horrific) explanation for the sightings and their associated smell. Apparently Sir John Wynn (either the 1st or the 5th Baronet – this remains unclear) seduced a serving maid at Gwydir in his youth. When the relationship became 'complicated', the unscrupulous Sir John murdered the girl and had her body walled up within a large void in one of the chimney-breasts. The smell of the decomposing

body, it is said, lingered for months as an unfortunate reminder of his former amour. Significantly, a hollowed-out space was found earlier this century within the chimney breast which backs onto the Ghost Room at the hall end of the passage. This, long called the 'priest hole', is where the body was said to have been secreted; and it is in this area that the smell is always at its strongest.

The 5th Baronet is said to have made a death-bed confession to a murder committed at Gwydir during his youth in the mid-seventeenth century. But the 1st Baronet (1553–1627) is an equally likely candidate for the girl's horrible murder. His (much exaggerated) reputation as a local tyrant was established already in local folklore when Thomas Pennant, the antiquary, visited the area in the 1770s. He recounts a tradition (which continues to this day) that the spirit of the old baronet remains trapped beneath the waterfall near Betws-y-Coed called Swallow Falls, 'forever to be purged, purified and spat upon (by the waters) for the evil deeds committed by him in his days of nature'.

Sir John himself ranks among the many other reported ghosts. He has been sighted on a number of occasions on the spiral staircase leading from the Solar Hall to the Great Chamber; his portrait hangs in the Lower Hall. A detailed account of all the other sightings would prove exhaustive, but among them children have been heard crying, and a ghost dog has frequently been seen (incredibly, its bones were unearthed in the cellar in 1995).

The Dutch Garden, from the north.

The gardens

The early gardens

The gardens at Gwydir are listed Grade 1 along with the house, and extend to around ten acres. As is usual with surviving early gardens, they represent something of a palimpsest, with early and later nineteenth-century elements overlaying those of the Tudor and Stuart periods. Records of a former moat and at least one fish pond probably relate to the earliest phases of formal landscaping. In addition, it is likely that the earliest house would have had – at the very least – one or more orchards associated with it. The survival, in the courtyard, of a fine mid-sixteenth-century garden arch – heraldically carved on both sides – indicates that some sort of garden enclosure or enclosures existed already in the time of John Wynn ap Meredith (d.1559), if not before.

The gardens from the south-east, c.1900, showing the 'Lovers' Tree'.

By the time of the 1st Baronet (1553–1627) the gardens are known to have been of some sophistication, with 'alleys and walks', a labyrinth and various garden structures recorded. The head gardener at this time was Owain Jeffreys, an able designer and topiarist, who was evidently held in high esteem. Oranges, lemons, figs, bay-trees and plums are among the exotica grown here, and 'pyramids and statuary' were sent up from London in 1617. A 'pleasure house' (1592), dovecote (1597) and bowling green are also mentioned, in addition to a deer park (1597), hop field (1593) and rabbit warren (1612), which specifically served the Gwydir table.

The nineteenth-century gardens

Much work was carried out in the gardens in the 1820s and 1830s under Peter Robert Burrell, 22nd Baron Willoughby de Eresby and 2nd Baron Gwydir, together with his wife Clementina. At the same time they commissioned similar work at their other houses, Grims-thorpe and Drummond castles. The famous garden and landscape designer Lewis Kennedy was responsible for undertaking the work at all three sites, where common themes (for example heraldic parterres, similar plantings and the use of white quartz) can be detected.

The main courtyard contains a large Knot Garden, originally conceived in the shape of a Tudor rose. This was laid out by Kennedy, who worked in collaboration with the architect Sir Charles Barry on Gwydir's restoration in the 1820s and 1830s. The wisteria on the Hall Range façade, together with the peacocks, are said to have been introduced at the same time as the Knot Garden, about 1828.

In 1901 *Country Life* published an article specifically on the gardens at Gwydir (followed, in 1908, by an article on the castle and its contents). By the mid-1990s the gardens were in a state of neglect and many areas had become overgrown. The restoration of the gardens has been undertaken concurrently with that of the house, and still continues. The terraces to the north-west of the Dutch Garden have now been restored, and a new 'Senses Garden' was created in the year 2000 adjacent to Sir John's Arch.

Sir John Wynn's Arch is an extraordinary survival from the renaissance gardens. Dating probably from the 1590s, it stands at the end of a long raised terrace. It bears the initials of Sir John and the three heraldic charges of the Wynn family.

Gwydir's notable trees

To the south-east, beyond the main courtyard, are two large and prominent cedar trees. These are two of the four remaining Cedars of Lebanon traditionally said to have been brought back from Spain as saplings by the 2nd Baronet, Sir Richard, when he accompanied Prince Charles on his ill-fated (and somewhat comical) attempt to woo the Infanta. Twelve trees were originally planted in 1625 to commemorate King Charles I's marriage to Queen Henrietta-Maria, whose treasurer Sir Richard subsequently became.

Within the present car park stands a large sycamore tree which is officially estimated to be over 400 years old. As such it appears to be the oldest of its kind in Wales. It stands near the site of the 1592 summerhouse (demolished c.1822). The lime tree nearby is, correspondingly, recorded as the tallest of its kind in the Principality.

Beyond the car-parking area are the Royal and Statesman's gardens. Here oak trees were planted during the royal visit of 1899, and again in 1911.

The Old Dutch Garden

To the north-west stretches the Old Dutch Garden, as it was called in the nineteenth century. This has six massive topiaried yews leading down to a central fountain. The fountain, surrounded by quartz boulders since the nine-

teenth century, has an octagonal basin of dressed slate-stone which appears to date to the time of the 1st Baronet in the early seventeenth century. The single fountain jet is gravity fed, the water supply originating at the top of the Grey Mare's Tail, a waterfall half-a-mile to the north-west. The water is channelled along a long rock-cut leat which curves around the contour of the partly wooded hillside above Gwydir before being piped down under the lane and into the garden. It has been suggested that this may be among the earliest operating fountains of its type in Wales.

The terraces to the west feature a further series of descending fountains, spouts and rills, culminating in a moated island with another, central fountain. The water employed here comes from the same source, the Grey Mare's Tail. Like that in the Dutch Garden, these fountains are therefore dependent on natural water pressure, rather than pumps.

*The Dutch Garden and fountain c.1860
(from a photograph by Francis Bedford).*